Non-Programmers Tutorial For Python 3

Josh Cogliati

March 31, 2019

Abstract

Non-Programmers Tutorial For Python 3 is a tutorial designed to be a introduction to the Python 3 programming language. This guide is for someone with no programming experience.

If you have programmed in other languages I recommend using The Python Tutorial written by Guido van Rossum.

This document is available as LaTeX, HTML, and PDF. Go to http://jjc.freeshell.org/easytut3/ to see all these forms.

If you have any questions or comments please contact me at jjc@sdf.lonestar.org I welcome questions and comments about this tutorial. I will try to answer any questions you have as best as I can.

Thanks go to Elizabeth Cogliati for complaining enough :) about the original tutorial (that is almost unusable for a non-programmer), for proofreading and for many ideas and comments on it. Thanks to Joe Oppegaard for writing all the exercises. Thanks also to James A. Brown, Hamish Lawson, Amos Satterlee, Gerald, Elissa, Quique and Annie Brewer. Thanks to everyone I have missed.

Dedicated to Elizabeth Cogliati

CONTENTS

Intro

1.1 First things first

So, you've never programmed before. As we go through this tutorial I will attempt to teach you how to program. There really is only one way to learn to program. **You** must read code and write code. I'm going to show you lots of code. You should type in code that I show you to see what happens. Play around with it and make changes. The worst that can happen is that it won't work. When I type in code it will be formatted like this:

```
##Python is easy to learn
print("Hello, World!")
```

That's so it is easy to distinguish from the other text. To make it confusing I will also print what the computer outputs in that same font.

The next step is to get a computer with Python 3 on it.

1.2 Installing Python

In order to program in Python you need the Python software. If you are on a Linux or BSD computer, you probably already have Python 3 installed (check your package manager for an installation package if you don't, or you can compile Python 3 from source code. IDLE may be in a separate package). If you are on a Windows or macOS computer you will need to install Python 3. To install Python, download the appropriate file for your computer from `http://www.python.org/download`. You will need Python 3.3 or newer for this tutorial.

1.3 Interactive Mode

From the command line, interactive mode can be gotten to by typing `python3` In Windows (assuming that Python is in the PATH), the command `python` is used instead. Alternatively, you can go into IDLE (also called the Python GUI). You should see a window that has some text like this:

```
Python 3.6.6 (default, Jul 19 2018, 14:25:17)
[GCC 8.1.1 20180712 (Red Hat 8.1.1-5)] on linux
Type "help", "copyright", "credits" or "license" for more information.
>>>
```

The >>> is Python's way of telling you that you are in interactive mode. In interactive mode what you type is immediately run. Try typing 1+1 in. Python will respond with 2. Interactive mode allows you to test out and see what

Python will do. If you ever feel you need to play with new Python statements go into interactive mode and try them out.

1.4   Creating and Running Programs

Go into IDLE if you are not already. Go to `File` then `New Window`. In this window type the following:

```
print("Hello, World!")
```

First save the program. Go to `File` then `Save`. Save it as `hello.py`. (If you want, you can save it to some other directory than the default.) Now that it is saved it can be run.

Next run the program by going to `Run` then `Run Module`. This will output `Hello, World!` on the `*Python Shell*` window.

Confused still? Try this tutorial for IDLE at `http://hkn.eecs.berkeley.edu/~dyoo/python/idle_intro/index.html`

1.5   Using Python from the command line

If you don't want to use Python from the command line, you don't have to, just use IDLE. For those of you who don't want to use IDLE, to get into interactive mode just type `python3` without any arguments (`python` in Windows). To run a program create it with a text editor (Emacs has a good python mode, Notepad++ also has a python mode) and then run it with `python3 program_name.py` (If in Windows, use `python program_name.py` in the cmd window from the correct directory).

Hello, World

2.1 What you should know

You should know how to edit programs in a text editor or IDLE, save them to disk (floppy or hard or flash) and run them once they have been saved.

2.2 Printing

Programming tutorials since the beginning of time have started with a little program called Hello, World! So here it is:

```
print("Hello, World!")
```

If you are using the command line to run programs then type it in with a text editor, save it as `hello.py` and run it with `python3 hello.py`

Otherwise go into IDLE, create a new window, and create the program as in section 1.4.

When this program is run here's what it prints:

```
Hello, World!
```

Now I'm not going to tell you this every time, but when I show you a program I recommend that you type it in and run it. I learn better when I type programs in and you probably do too.

Now here is a more complicated program:

```
print("Jack and Jill went up a hill")
print("to fetch a pail of water;")
print("Jack fell down, and broke his crown,")
print("and Jill came tumbling after.")
```

When you run this program it prints out:

```
Jack and Jill went up a hill
to fetch a pail of water;
Jack fell down, and broke his crown,
and Jill came tumbling after.
```

When the computer runs this program, first it sees the line:

```
print("Jack and Jill went up a hill")
```

so the computer prints:

```
Jack and Jill went up a hill
```

Then the computer goes down to the next line and sees:

```
print("to fetch a pail of water;")
```

So the computer prints to the screen:

```
to fetch a pail of water;
```

The computer keeps looking at each line, follows the command, and then goes on to the next line. The computer keeps running commands until it reaches the end of the program.

2.3 Expressions

Here is another program:

```
print("2 + 2 is", 2+2)
print("3 * 4 is", 3 * 4)
print(100 - 1, " = 100 - 1")
print("(33 + 2) / 5 + 11.5 = ", (33 + 2) / 5 + 11.5)
```

And here is the output when the program is run:

```
2 + 2 is 4
3 * 4 is 12
99  = 100 - 1
(33 + 2) / 5 + 11.5 =   18.5
```

As you can see, Python can turn your thousand dollar computer into a 5 dollar calculator.

Python has seven basic operations for numbers:[1]

Operation	Symbol	Example
Exponentiation	**	5 ** 2 == 25
Multiplication	*	2 * 3 == 6
Division	/	15 / 2 == 7.5
Integer Division	//	14 // 3 == 4
Remainder	%	14 % 3 == 2
Addition	+	1 + 2 == 3
Subtraction	−	4 − 3 == 1

Notice that there are two different division rules. If you use // then it returns the integer result (15 // 2 == 7). If you use / then it returns the decimal result (15 / 2 == 7.5). The following program show this:

```
print("15 / 2 = ", 15 / 2)
print("15 // 2 = ", 15 // 2)
```

---

[1]I used == because in Python == is used for testing if two things are equal.

```
print("15 % 2 = ", 15 % 2)
print()
print("15.0 / 2.0 =", 15.0 / 2.0)
print("15.0 // 2.0 =", 15.0 // 2.0)
print("15.0 % 2.0 =", 15 % 2.0)
print()
```

With the output:

```
15 / 2 =  7.5
15 // 2 =  7
15 % 2 =  1

15.0 / 2.0 = 7.5
15.0 // 2.0 = 7.0
15.0 % 2.0 = 1.0
```

The order of operations is the same as in math:

1. parentheses ()

2. exponents **

3. multiplication *, division \, integer division \ \, and remainder %

4. addition + and subtraction −

2.4   Talking to humans (and other intelligent beings)

Often in programming you are doing something complicated and may not in the future remember what you did. When this happens the program should probably be commented. A comment is a note to you and other programmers explaining what is happening. For example:

```
#Not quite PI, but an incredible simulation
print(22/7)
```

Notice that the comment starts with a # and lasts till the end of the line. Comments are used to communicate with others who read the program and your future self to make clear what is complicated.

2.5   Examples

Most chapters contain examples of the programming features introduced in the chapter. You should at least look over them to see if you understand them. If you don't, you may want to type them in and see what happens. Mess around with them, change them, and see what happens.

Denmark.py

```
print("Something's rotten in the state of Denmark.")
print("                -- Shakespeare")
```

Output:

```
Something's rotten in the state of Denmark.
              -- Shakespeare
```

School.py

```
#This is not quite true outside of USA
# and is based on my dim memories of my younger years
print("Firstish Grade")
print("1+1 =", 1+1)
print("2+4 =", 2+4)
print("5-2 =", 5-2)
print()
print("Thirdish Grade")
print("243-23 =", 243-23)
print("12*4 =", 12*4)
print("12/3 =", 12//3)
print("13/3 =", 13//3, "R", 13%3)
print()
print("Junior High")
print("123.25-62.75 =", 123.25-62.75)
print("(4+3)*2 =", (4+3)*2)
print("4+3*2 =", 4+3*2)
print("3**2 =", 3**2)
print()
```

Output:

```
Firstish Grade
1+1 = 2
2+4 = 6
5-2 = 3

Thirdish Grade
243-23 = 220
12*4 = 48
12/3 = 4
13/3 = 4 R 1

Junior High
123.25-62.75 = 60.5
(4+3)*2 = 14
4+3*2 = 10
3**2 = 9
```

2.6 Exercises

Write a program that prints your full name and your birthday as separate strings.

Write a program that shows the use of at least 4 of the 7 math functions.

Who Goes There?

3.1 Input and Variables

Now I feel it is time for a really complicated program. Here it is:

```
print("Halt!")
s = input("Who Goes there? ")
print("You may pass,", s)
```

When **I** ran it here is what **my** screen showed:

```
Halt!
Who Goes there? Josh
You may pass, Josh
```

Of course when you run the program your screen will look different because of the `input` statement. When you ran the program you probably noticed (you did run the program, right?) how you had to type in your name and then press Enter. Then the program printed out some more text and also your name. This is an example of input. The program reaches a certain point and then waits for the user to input some data that the program can use later.

Of course, getting information from the user would be useless if we didn't have anywhere to put that information and this is where variables come in. In the previous program `s` is a variable. Variables are like a box that can store some piece of data. Here is a program to show examples of variables:

```
a = 123.4
b23 = 'Spam'
first_name = "Bill"
b = 432
c = a + b
print("a + b is", c)
print("first_name is", first_name)
print("Sorted Parts, After Midnight or", b23)
```

And here is the output:

```
a + b is 555.4
first_name is Bill
Sorted Parts, After Midnight or Spam
```

Variables store data. The variables in the above program are `a`, `b23`, `first_name`, `b`, and `c`. The two basic types are strings and numbers. Strings are a sequence of letters, numbers and other characters. In this example `b23` and `first_name` are variables that are storing strings. `Spam`, `Bill`, `a + b is`, and `first_name is` are the strings in this program. The characters are surrounded by `"` or `'`. The other type of variables are numbers.[1]

Okay, so we have these boxes called variables and also data that can go into the variable. The computer will see a line like `first_name = "Bill"` and it reads it as Put the string `Bill` into the box (or variable) `first_name`. Later on it sees the statement `c = a + b` and it reads it as Put `a + b` or `123.4 + 432` or `555.4` into `c`.

Here is another example of variable usage:

```
a = 1
print(a)
a = a + 1
print(a)
a = a * 2
print(a)
```

And of course here is the output:

```
1
2
4
```

Even if it is the same variable on both sides the computer still reads it as: First find out the data to store and than find out where the data goes.

One more program before I end this chapter:

```
num = float(input("Type in a Number: "))
str = input("Type in a String: ")
print("num =", num)
print("num is a ", type(num))
print("num * 2 =", num*2)
print("str =", str)
print("str is a ", type(str))
print("str * 2 =", str*2)
```

The output I got was:

```
Type in a Number: 12.34
Type in a String: Hello
num = 12.34
num is a  <class 'float'>
num * 2 = 24.68
str = Hello
str is a  <class 'str'>
str * 2 = HelloHello
```

Notice that `num` was gotten with `float(input(...))` while `str` was gotten with `input`. `input` returns a string and the function `float` converts it to a floating point number. There is also a function `int` that converts a string or a floating point number into an integer.

The second half of the program uses `type` which tells what a variable is. Numbers are of type `int` or `float` (which are short for 'integer' and 'floating point' respectively). Strings are of type `string`. Integers and floats can be worked on by mathematical functions, strings cannot. Notice how when python multiples a number by a integer the expected

---

[1] Python allows more types of variables. For example, later in the tutorial we will learn about lists and functions.

thing happens. However when a string is multiplied by a integer the string has that many copies of it repeated: for example `str * 2 = HelloHello`.

The operations with strings do slightly different things than operations with numbers. Here are some interative mode examples to show that some more.

```
>>> "This"+" "+"is"+" joined."
'This is joined.'
>>> "Ha, "*5
'Ha, Ha, Ha, Ha, Ha, '
>>> "Ha, "*5+"ha!"
'Ha, Ha, Ha, Ha, Ha, ha!'
>>>
```

Here is the list of some string operations:

Operation	Symbol	Example
Repetition	*	`"i"*5 == "iiiii"`
Concatenation	+	`"Hello, "+"World!" == "Hello, World!"`

3.2 Examples

Rate_times.py

```
#This programs calculates rate and distance problems
print("Input a rate and a distance")
rate = float(input("Rate:"))
distance = float(input("Distance:"))
print("Time:", distance/rate)
```

Sample runs:

```
> python3 rate_times.py
Input a rate and a distance
Rate:5
Distance:10
Time: 2.0
> python3 rate_times.py
Input a rate and a distance
Rate:3.52
Distance:45.6
Time: 12.9545454545
```

Area.py

```
#This program calculates the perimeter and area of a rectangle
print("Calculate information about a rectangle")
length = float(input("Length:"))
width = float(input("Width:"))
print("Area", length*width)
print("Perimeter", 2*length+2*width)
```

Sample runs:

```
> python3 area.py
Calculate information about a rectangle
Length:4
Width:3
Area 12.0
Perimeter 14.0
> python3 area.py
Calculate information about a rectangle
Length:2.53
Width:5.2
Area 13.156
Perimeter 15.46
```

temperature.py

```
#Converts Fahrenheit to Celsius
temp = float(input("Farenheit temperature:"))
print((temp-32.0)*5.0/9.0)
```

Sample runs:

```
> python3 temperature.py
Farenheit temperature:32
0.0
> python3 temperature.py
Farenheit temperature:-40
-40.0
> python3 temperature.py
Farenheit temperature:212
100.0
> python3 temperature.py
Farenheit temperature:98.6
37.0
```

3.3 Exercises

Write a program that gets 2 string variables and 2 integer variables from the user, concatenates (joins them together with no spaces) and displays the strings, then multiplies the two numbers on a new line.

Count to 10

4.1 While loops

Presenting our first control structure. Ordinarily, the computer starts with the first line and then goes down from there. Control structures change the order that statements are executed or decide if a certain statement will be run. Here's the source for a program that uses the while control structure:

```
a = 0
while a < 10:
    a = a + 1
    print(a)
```

And here is the extremely exciting output:

```
1
2
3
4
5
6
7
8
9
10
```

(And you thought it couldn't get any worse after turning your computer into a five dollar calculator?) So what does the program do? First it sees the line a = 0 and makes a zero. Then it sees while a < 10: and so the computer checks to see if a < 10. The first time the computer sees this statement a is zero so it is less than 10. In other words while a is less than ten the computer will run the indented statements.

Here is another example of the use of while:

```
a = 1
s = 0
print('Enter Numbers to add to the sum.')
print('Enter 0 to quit.')
while a != 0:
    print('Current Sum:', s)
    a = float(input('Number? '))
    s = s + a
print('Total Sum =', s)
```

The first time I ran this program Python printed out:

```
  File "sum.py", line 3
    while a != 0
                ^
SyntaxError: invalid syntax
```

I had forgotten to put the : after the while. The error message complained about that problem and pointed out where it thought the problem was with the ^ . After the problem was fixed here was what I did with the program:

```
Enter Numbers to add to the sum.
Enter 0 to quit.
Current Sum: 0
Number? 200
Current Sum: 200.0
Number? -15.25
Current Sum: 184.75
Number? -151.85
Current Sum: 32.9
Number? 10.00
Current Sum: 42.9
Number? 0
Total Sum = 42.9
```

Notice how print('Total Sum =', s) is only run at the end. The while statement only affects the line that are indented (a.k.a. have spaces at the front). The != means does not equal so while a != 0: means until a is zero run the indented statements that are afterwards. (Note: be consistent, always use spaces or tabs to indent, never mix them.)

Now that we have while loops, it is possible to have programs that run forever. An easy way to do this is to write a program like this:

```
while 1 == 1:
    print("Help, I'm stuck in a loop.")
```

This program will output Help, I'm stuck in a loop. until the heat death of the universe or you stop it. The way to stop it is to hit the Control (or Ctrl) button and 'c' (the letter) at the same time. This will kill the program. (Note: sometimes you will have to hit enter after the Control C.)

4.2 Examples

Fibonnacci.py

```
#This program calulates the fibonnacci sequence
a = 0
b = 1
count = 0
max_count = 20
while count < max_count:
    count = count + 1
    #we need to keep track of a since we change it
    old_a = a
```

```
        old_b = b
        a = old_b
        b = old_a + old_b
        #Notice that end=' ' in a print statement keeps it
        # from switching to a new line
        print(old_a, end=' ')
print()
```

Output:

```
0 1 1 2 3 5 8 13 21 34 55 89 144 233 377 610 987 1597 2584 4181
```

Password.py

```
# Waits until a password has been entered.  Use control-C to break out with out
# the password

#Note that this must not be the password so that the
# while loop runs at least once.
password = "something else"

#note that != means not equal
while password != "unicorn":
    password = input("Password:")
print("Welcome in")
```

Sample run:

```
Password:auo
Password:y22
Password:password
Password:open sesame
Password:unicorn
Welcome in
```

Decisions

5.1 If statement

As always I believe I should start each chapter with a warm up typing exercise so here is a short program to compute the absolute value of a number:

```
n = float(input("Number? "))
if n < 0:
    print("The absolute value of", n, "is", -n)
else:
    print("The absolute value of", n, "is", n)
```

Here is the output from the two times that I ran this program:

```
Number? -34
The absolute value of -34.0 is 34.0

Number? 1
The absolute value of 1.0 is 1.0
```

So what does the computer do when when it sees this piece of code? First it prompts the user for a number with the statement `n = float(input("Number?   "))`. Next it reads the line `if n < 0:`. If n is less than zero Python runs the line `print("The absolute value of", n, "is", -n)`. Otherwise python runs the line `print("The absolute value of", n, "is", n)`.

More formally Python looks at whether the *expression* `n < 0` is true or false. A `if` statement is followed by a *block* of statements that are run when the expression is true. Optionally after the `if` statement is a `else` statement. The `else` statement is run if the expression is false.

There are several different tests that a expression can have. Here is a table of all of them:

operator	function
<	less than
<=	less than or equal to
>	greater than
>=	greater than or equal to
==	equal
!=	not equal

Another feature of the `if` command is the `elif` statement. It stands for else if and means if the original `if` statement is false and then the `elif` part is true do that part. Here's a example:

```
a = 0
```

```
while a < 10:
    a = a + 1
    if a > 5:
        print(a, " > ", 5)
    elif a <= 7:
        print(a, " <= ", 7)
    else:
        print("Neither test was true")
```

and the output:

```
1   <=  7
2   <=  7
3   <=  7
4   <=  7
5   <=  7
6   >   5
7   >   5
8   >   5
9   >   5
10  >   5
```

Notice how the `elif a <= 7` is only tested when the `if` statement fail to be true. `elif` allows multiple tests to be done in a single if statement.

5.2   Examples

High_low.py

```
#Plays the guessing game higher or lower
# (originally written by Josh Cogliati, improved by Quique)

#This should actually be something that is semi random like the
# last digits of the time or something else, but that will have to
# wait till a later chapter.  (Extra Credit, modify it to be random
# after the Modules chapter)
number = 78
guess = 0

while guess != number:
    guess = int(input("Guess a number: "))

    if guess > number:
        print("Too high")

    elif guess < number:
        print("Too low")

print("Just right")
```

Sample run:

```
Guess a number:100
Too high
Guess a number:50
Too low
Guess a number:75
Too low
Guess a number:87
Too high
Guess a number:81
Too high
Guess a number:78
Just right
```

even.py

```
#Asks for a number.
#Prints if it is even or odd

number = float(input("Tell me a number: "))
if number % 2 == 0:
    print(number, "is even.")
elif number % 2 == 1:
    print(number, "is odd.")
else:
    print(number, "is very strange.")
```

Sample runs.

```
Tell me a number: 3
3.0 is odd.

Tell me a number: 2
2.0 is even.

Tell me a number: 3.14159
3.14159 is very strange.
```

average1.py

```
#keeps asking for numbers until 0 is entered.
#Prints the average value.

count = 0
sum = 0.0
number = 1 #set this to something that will not exit
#          the while loop immediatly.

print("Enter 0 to exit the loop")

while number != 0:
    number = float(input("Enter a number:"))
    count = count + 1
    sum = sum + number
```

```
count = count - 1 #take off one for the last number
print("The average was:", sum/count)
```

Sample runs

```
Enter 0 to exit the loop
Enter a number:3
Enter a number:5
Enter a number:0
The average was: 4.0

Enter 0 to exit the loop
Enter a number:1
Enter a number:4
Enter a number:3
Enter a number:0
The average was: 2.66666666667
```

average2.py

```
#keeps asking for numbers until count have been entered.
#Prints the average value.

sum = 0.0

print("This program will take several numbers then average them")
count = int(input("How many numbers would you like to sum:"))
current_count = 0

while current_count < count:
    current_count = current_count + 1
    print("Number ", current_count)
    number = float(input("Enter a number:"))
    sum = sum + number

print("The average was:", sum/count)
```

Sample runs

```
This program will take several numbers then average them
How many numbers would you like to sum:2
Number  1
Enter a number:3
Number  2
Enter a number:5
The average was: 4.0

This program will take several numbers then average them
How many numbers would you like to sum:3
Number  1
Enter a number:1
Number  2
Enter a number:4
Number  3
```

```
Enter a number:3
The average was: 2.66666666667
```

5.3 Exercises

Modify the password guessing program to keep track of how many times the user has entered the password wrong. If it is more than 3 times, print "That must have been complicated."

Write a program that asks for two numbers. If the sum of the numbers is greater than 100, print "That is big number".

Write a program that asks the user their name, if they enter your name say "That is a nice name", if they enter "John Cleese" or "Michael Palin", tell them how you feel about them ;), otherwise tell them "You have a nice name".

Debugging

6.1 What is debugging?

> As soon as we started programming, we found to our surprise that it wasn't as easy to get programs right as we had thought. Debugging had to be discovered. I can remember the exact instant when I realized that a large part of my life from then on was going to be spent in finding mistakes in my own programs.
> – Maurice Wilkes discovers debugging, 1949

By now if you have been messing around with the programs you have probably found that sometimes the program does something you didn't want it to do. This is fairly common. Debugging is the process of figuring out what the computer is doing and then getting it to do what you want it to do. This can be tricky. I once spent nearly a week tracking down and fixing a bug that was caused by someone putting an x where a y should have been.

This chapter will be more abstract than previous chapters. Some people find it useful, others don't.

6.2 What should the program do?

The first thing to do (this sounds obvious) is to figure out what the program should be doing if it is running correctly. Come up with some test cases and see what happens. For example, let's say I have a program to compute the perimeter of a rectangle (the sum of the length of all the edges). I have the following test cases:

width	height	perimeter
3	4	14
2	3	10
4	4	16
2	2	8
5	1	12

I now run my program on all of the test cases and see if the program does what I expect it to do. If it doesn't then I need to find out what the computer is doing.

More commonly some of the test cases will work and some will not. If that is the case you should try and figure out what the working ones have in common. For example here is the output for a perimeter program (you get to see the code in a minute):

```
Height: 3
Width: 4
perimeter =  15.0


Height: 2
```

```
Width: 3
perimeter =   11.0

Height: 4
Width: 4
perimeter =   16.0

Height: 2
Width: 2
perimeter =   8.0

Height: 5
Width: 1
perimeter =   8.0
```

Notice that it didn't work for the first two inputs, it worked for the next two and it didn't work on the last one. Try and figure out what is in common with the working ones. Once you have some idea what the problem is finding the cause is easier. With your own programs you should try more test cases if you need them.

6.3 What does the program do?

The next thing to do is to look at the source code. One of the most important things to do while programming is reading source code. The primary way to do this is code walkthroughs.

A code walkthrough starts at the first line, and works its way down until the program is done. `While` loops and `if` statements mean that some lines may never be run and some lines are run many times. At each line you figure out what Python has done.

Lets start with the simple perimeter program. Don't type it in, you are going to read it, not run it. The source code is:

```
height = float(input("Height: "))
width = float(input("Width: "))
print("perimeter = ", width+height+width+width)
```

Question: What is the first line Python runs?

Answer: The first line is alway run first. For this program, it is:
`height = float(input("Height: "))`

Question: What does that line do?

Answer: Prints `Height:`   , waits for the user to type a line in, and then converts it to a number, and puts that in the variable height.

Question: What is the next line that runs?

Answer: In general, it is the next line down which is: `width = float(input("Width: "))`

Question: What does that line do?

Answer: Prints `Width:`   , waits for the user to type a number in, and puts what the user types in the variable width.

Question: What is the next line that runs?

Answer: When the next line is not indented more or less than the current line, it is the line right afterwards, so it is:
`print("perimeter = ", width+height+width+width)`

Question: What does that line do?

Answer: First it prints `perimeter =`, then it prints `width+height+width+width`.

Question: Does `width+height+width+width` calculate the perimeter properly?

Answer: Let's see, perimeter of a rectangle is the bottom (width) plus the left side (height) plus the top (width) plus the right side (huh?). The last item should be the right side's length, or the height.

Question: Do you understand why some of the times the perimeter was calculated 'correctly'?

Answer: It was calculated correctly when the width and the height were equal.

The next program we will do a code walkthrough for is a program that is supposed to print out 5 dots on the screen. However, this is what the program is outputting:

```
.  .  .  .
```

And here is the program:

```
number = 5
while number > 1:
    print(".", end=" ")
    number = number - 1
print()
```

This program will be more complex to walkthrough since it now has indented portions (or control structures). Let us begin.

Question: What is the first line to be run?

Answer: The first line of the file: `number = 5`

Question: What does it do?

Answer: Puts the number 5 in the variable `number`.

Question: What is the next line?

Answer: The next line is: `while number > 1:`

Question: What does it do?

Answer: Well, `while` statements in general look at their expression, and if it is true they do the next indented block of code, otherwise they skip the next indented block of code.

Question: So what does it do right now?

Answer: If `number > 1` is true then the next two lines will be run.

Question: So is `number > 1`?

Answer: The last value put into `number` was 5 and `5 > 1` so yes.

Question: So what is the next line?

Answer: Since the `while` was true the next line is: `print(".", end=" ")`

Question: What does that line do?

Answer: Prints one dot and since the function includes `end=" "` the next print statement will not be on a different screen line.

Question: What is the next line?

Answer: `number = number - 1` since that is following line and there are no indent changes.

Question: What does it do?

Answer: It calculates `number - 1`, which is the current value of `number` (or 5) subtracts 1 from it, and makes that the new value of `number`. So basically it changes `number`'s value from 5 to 4.

Question: What is the next line?

Answer: Well, the indent level decreases so we have to look at what type of control structure it is. It is a `while` loop, so we have to go back to the `while` clause which is `while number > 1:`

Question: What does it do?

Answer: It looks at the value of `number`, which is 4, and compares it to 1 and since `4 > 1` the while loop continues.

Question: What is the next line?

Answer: Since the while loop was true, the next line is: `print(".", end=" ")`

Question: What does it do?

Answer: It prints a second dot on the line.

Question: What is the next line?

Answer: No indent change so it is: `number = number - 1`

Question: And what does it do?

Answer: It talks the current value of `number` (4), subtracts 1 from it, which gives it 3 and then finally makes 3 the new value of `number`.

Question: What is the next line?

Answer: Since there is an indent change caused by the end of the while loop, the next line is: `while number > 1:`

Question: What does it do?

Answer: It compares the current value of `number` (3) to 1. `3 > 1` so the while loop continues.

Question: What is the next line?

Answer: Since the while loop condition was true the next line is: `print(".", end=" ")`

Question: And it does what?

Answer: A third dot is printed on the line.

Question: What is the next line?

Answer: It is: `number = number - 1`

Question: What does it do?

Answer: It takes the current value of `number` (3) subtracts from it 1 and makes the 2 the new value of `number`.

Question: What is the next line?

Answer: Back up to the start of the while loop: `while number > 1:`

Question: What does it do?

Answer: It compares the current value of `number` (2) to 1. Since `2 > 1` the while loop continues.

Question: What is the next line?

Answer: Since the while loop is continuing: `print(".", end=" ")`

Question: What does it do?

Answer: It discovers the meaning of life, the universe, and everything. I'm joking. (I had to make sure you were awake.) The line prints a fourth dot on the screen.

Question: What is the next line?

Answer: It's: `number = number - 1`

Question: What does it do?

Answer: Takes the current value of `number` (2) subtracts 1 and makes 1 the new value of `number`.

Question: What is the next line?

Answer: Back up to the while loop: `while number > 1:`

Question: What does the line do?

Answer: It compares the current value of `number` (1) to 1. Since `1 > 1` is false (one is not greater than one), the while loop exits.

Question: What is the next line?

Answer: Since the while loop condition was false the next line is the line after the while loop exits, or: `print()`

Question: What does that line do?

Answer: Makes the screen go to the next line.

Question: Why doesn't the program print 5 dots?

Answer: The loop exits 1 dot too soon.

Question: How can we fix that?

Answer: Make the loop exit 1 dot later.

Question: And how do we do that?

Answer: There are several ways. One way would be to change the while loop to: `while number > 0:`. Another way would be to change the conditional to: `number >= 1` There are a couple others.

6.4 How do I fix the program?

You need to figure out what the program is doing. You need to figure out what the program should do. Figure out what the difference between the two is. Debugging is a skill that has to be done to be learned. If you can't figure it out after an hour or so take a break, talk to someone about the problem, or contemplate the lint in your navel. Come back in a while and you will probably have new ideas about the problem. Good luck.

Defining Functions

7.1 Creating Functions

To start off this chapter I am going to give you a example of what you could do but shouldn't (so don't type it in):

```
a = 23
b = -23

if a < 0:
    a = -a

if b < 0:
    b = -b

if a == b:
    print("The absolute values of", a, "and", b, "are equal")
else:
    print("The absolute values of a and b are different")
```

with the output being:

```
The absolute values of 23 and 23 are equal
```

The program seems a little repetitive. (Programmers hate to repeat things (That's what computers are for aren't they?)) Fortunately Python allows you to create functions to remove duplication. Here's the rewritten example:

```
a = 23
b = -23

def my_abs(num):
    if num < 0:
        num = -num
    return num

if my_abs(a) == my_abs(b):
    print("The absolute values of", a, "and", b, "are equal")
else:
    print("The absolute values of a and b are different")
```

with the output being:

```
The absolute values of 23 and -23 are equal
```

The key feature of this program is the def statement. def (short for define) starts a function definition. def is followed by the name of the function my_abs. Next comes a (followed by the parameter num (num is passed from the program into the function when the function is called). The statements after the : are executed when the function is used. The statements continue until either the indented statements end or a return is encountered. The return statement returns a value back to the place where the function was called.

Notice how the values of a and b are not changed. Functions of course can be used to repeat tasks that don't return values. Here's some examples:

```
def hello():
    print("Hello")

def area(width, height):
    return width*height

def print_welcome(name):
    print("Welcome", name)

hello()
hello()

print_welcome("Fred")
w = 4
h = 5
print("width =", w, "height =", h, "area =", area(w, h))
```

with output being:

```
Hello
Hello
Welcome Fred
width = 4 height = 5 area = 20
```

That example just shows some more stuff that you can do with functions. Notice that you can use no arguments or two or more. Notice also when a function doesn't need to send back a value, a return is optional.

7.2   Variables in functions

Of course, when eliminiating repeated code, you often have variables in the repeated code. These are dealt with in a special way in Python. Up till now, all variables we have see are global variables. Functions have a special type of variable called local variables. These variables only exist while the function is running. When a local variable has the same name as another variable such as a global variable, the local variable hides the other variable. Sound confusing? Well, hopefully this next example (which is a bit contrived) will clear things up.

```
a_var = 10
b_var = 15
e_var = 25

def a_func(a_var):
    print("in a_func a_var = ", a_var)
```

```
    b_var = 100 + a_var
    d_var = 2*a_var
    print("in a_func b_var = ", b_var)
    print("in a_func d_var = ", d_var)
    print("in a_func e_var = ", e_var)
    return b_var + 10

c_var = a_func(b_var)

print("a_var = ", a_var)
print("b_var = ", b_var)
print("c_var = ", c_var)
print("d_var = ", d_var)
```

The output is:

```
in a_func a_var =   15
in a_func b_var =   115
in a_func d_var =   30
in a_func e_var =   25
a_var =   10
b_var =   15
c_var =   125
Traceback (most recent call last):
  File "varfunc.py", line 19, in <module>
    print("d_var = ", d_var)
NameError: name 'd_var' is not defined
```

In this example the variables a_var, b_var, and d_var are all local variables when they are inside the function a_func. After the statement return b_var + 10 is run, they all cease to exist. The variable a_var is automatically a local variable since it is a parameter name. The variables b_var and d_var are local variables since they appear on the left of an equals sign in the function in the statements b_var = 100 + a_var and d_var = 2*a_var.

Inside of the function a_var is 15 since the function is called with a_func(b_var). Since at that point in time b_var is 15, the call to the function is a_func(15) This ends up setting a_var to 15 when it is inside of a_func.

As you can see, once the function finishes running, the local variables a_var and b_var that had hidden the global variables of the same name are gone. Then the statement print("a_var = ", a_var) prints the value 10 rather than the value 15 since the local variable that hid the global variable is gone.

Another thing to notice is the NameError that happens at the end. This appears since the variable d_var no longer exists since a_func finished. All the local variables are deleted when the function exits. If you want to get something from a function, then you will have to use return something.

One last thing to notice is that the value of e_var remains unchanged inside a_func since it is not a parameter and it never appears on the left of an equals sign inside of the function a_func. When a global variable is accessed inside a function it is the global variable from the outside.

Functions allow local variables that exist only inside the function and can hide other variables that are outside the function.

7.3   Function walkthrough

Now we will do a walk through for the following program:

```
def mult(a, b):
    if b == 0:
        return 0
    rest = mult(a, b - 1)
    value = a + rest
    return value

print("3*2 = ", mult(3, 2))
```

Basically, this program creates a positive integer multiplication function (that is far slower than the built in multiplication function) and then demonstrates this function with a use of the function. Some people find this section helpful, others find it confusing. If it gets confusing, you can skip it.

Question: What is the first thing the program does?

Answer: The first thing done is the function `mult` is defined with the lines:

```
def mult(a, b):
    if b == 0:
        return 0
    rest = mult(a, b - 1)
    value = a + rest
    return value
```

This creates a function that takes two parameters and returns a value when it is done. Later this function can be run.

Question: What happens next?

Answer: The next line after the function, `print("3*2 = ", mult(3, 2))` is run.

Question: And what does this do?

Answer: It prints `3*2 =` and the return value of `mult(3, 2)`

Question: And what does `mult(3, 2)` return?

Answer: We need to do a walkthrough of the `mult` function to find out.

Question: What happens next?

Answer: The variable a gets the value 3 assigned to it and the variable b gets the value 2 assigned to it.

Question: And then?

Answer: The line `if b == 0:` is run. Since b has the value 2 this is false so the line `return 0` is skipped.

Question: And what then?

Answer: The line `rest = mult(a, b - 1)` is run. This line sets the local variable `rest` to the value of `mult(a, b - 1)`. The value of a is 3 and the value of b is 2 so the function call is `mult(3, 1)`

Question: So what is the value of `mult(3, 1)` ?

Answer: We will need to run the function `mult` with the parameters 3 and 1.

Question: So what happens next?

Answer: The local variables in the *new* run of the function are set so that a has the value 3 and b has the value 1. Since these are local values these do not affect the previous values of a and b.

Question: And then?

Answer: Since b has the value 1 the if statement is false, so the next line becomes `rest = mult(a, b - 1)`.

Question: What does this line do?

Answer: This line will assign the value of `mult(3, 0)` to rest.

Question: So what is that value?

Answer: We will have to run the function one more time to find that out. This time a has the value 3 and b has the value 0.

Question: So what happens next?

Answer: The first line in the function to run is `if b == 0:`. b has the value 0 so the next line to run is `return 0`

Question: And what does the line `return 0` do?

Answer: This line returns the value 0 out of the function.

Question: So?

Answer: So now we know that `mult(3, 0)` has the value 0. Now we know what the line `rest = mult(a, b - 1)` did since we have run the function `mult` with the parameters 3 and 0. We have finished running `mult(3, 0)` and are now back to running `mult(3, 1)`. The variable `rest` gets assigned the value 0.

Question: What line is run next?

Answer: The line `value = a + rest` is run next. In this run of the function, a=3 and rest=0 so now value=3.

Question: What happens next?

Answer: The line `return value` is run. This returns 3 from the function. This also exits from the run of the function `mult(3, 1)`. After `return` is called, we go back to running `mult(3, 2)`.

Question: Where were we in `mult(3, 2)`?

Answer: We had the variables a=3 and b=2 and were examining the line `rest = mult(a, b - 1)`.

Question: So what happens now?

Answer: The variable `rest` get 3 assigned to it. The next line `value = a + rest` sets `value` to 3+3 or 6.

Question: So now what happens?

Answer: The next line runs, this returns 6 from the function. We are now back to running the line `print("3*2 = ", mult(3, 2))` which can now print out the 6.

Question: What is happening overall?

Answer: Basically, we used two facts to calulate the multiple of the two numbers. The first is that any number times 0 is 0 ($x * 0 = 0$). The second is that a number times another number is equal to the first number plus the first number times one less than the second number ($x * y = x + x * (y - 1)$). So what happens is $3*2$ is first converted into $3 + 3*1$. Then $3*1$ is converted into $3 + 3*0$. Then we know that any number times 0 is 0 so $3*0$ is 0. Then we can calculate that $3 + 3*0$ is $3 + 0$ which is 3. Now we know what $3*1$ is so we can calculate that $3 + 3*1$ is $3 + 3$ which is 6.

This is how the whole thing works:

```
3*2
3 + 3*1
3 + 3 + 3*0
3 + 3 + 0
3 + 3
6
```

Congratulations, you stepped through a complicated function.

7.4 Examples

factorial.py

```
#defines a function that calculates the factorial

def factorial(n):
    if n <= 1:
        return 1
    return n*factorial(n-1)

print("2! = ", factorial(2))
print("3! = ", factorial(3))
print("4! = ", factorial(4))
print("5! = ", factorial(5))
print("52! = ", factorial(52))
```

Output:

```
2! =  2
3! =  6
4! =  24
5! =  120
52! =  80658175170943878571660636856403766975289505440883277824000000000000
```

temperature2.py

```
#converts temperature to fahrenheit or celsius

def print_options():
    print("Options:")
    print(" 'p' print options")
    print(" 'c' convert from celsius")
    print(" 'f' convert from fahrenheit")
    print(" 'q' quit the program")

def celsius_to_fahrenheit(c_temp):
    return 9.0/5.0*c_temp+32

def fahrenheit_to_celsius(f_temp):
    return (f_temp - 32.0)*5.0/9.0

choice = "p"
while choice != "q":
    if choice == "c":
        temp = float(input("Celsius temperature:"))
        print("Fahrenheit:", celsius_to_fahrenheit(temp))
    elif choice == "f":
        temp = float(input("Fahrenheit temperature:"))
        print("Celsius:", fahrenheit_to_celsius(temp))
    elif choice != "q":
        print_options()
    choice = input("option:")
```

Sample Run:

```
> python3 temperature2.py
Options:
 'p' print options
 'c' convert from celsius
 'f' convert from fahrenheit
 'q' quit the program
option:c
Celsius temperature:30
Fahrenheit: 86.0
option:f
Fahrenheit temperature:60
Celsius: 15.5555555556
option:q
```

area2.py

```
#By Amos Satterlee
print()
def hello():
    print('Hello!')

def area(width, height):
    return width*height

def print_welcome(name):
    print('Welcome,', name)

def get_positive(prompt):
    value = float(input(prompt))
    while value <= 0:
        print('Must be a positive number')
        value = float(input(prompt))
    return value

name = input('Your Name: ')
hello()
print_welcome(name)
print()
print('To find the area of a rectangle,')
print('Enter the width and height below.')
print()
w = get_positive('Width:  ')
h = get_positive('Height: ')
print('Width =', w, ' Height =', h, ' so Area =', area(w, h))
```

Sample Run:

```
Your Name: Josh
Hello!
Welcome, Josh
```

```
To find the area of a rectangle,
Enter the width and height below.

Width:  -4
Must be a positive number
Width:  4
Height: 3
Width = 4.0  Height = 3.0  so Area = 12.0
```

7.5 Exercises

Rewrite the area.py program done in 3.2 to have a separate function for the area of a square, the area of a rectangle, and the area of a circle. (The area of a circle is roughly 3.14 * radius**2). This program should include a menu interface.

Lists

8.1   Variables with more than one value

You have already seen ordinary variables that store a single value. However other variable types can hold more than one value. The simplest type is called a list. Here is a example of a list being used:

```
which_one = int(input("What month (1-12)? "))
months = ['January', 'February', 'March', 'April', 'May', 'June', 'July',\
          'August', 'September', 'October', 'November', 'December']
if 1 <= which_one <= 12:
    print("The month is", months[which_one - 1])
```

and a output example:

```
What month (1-12)? 3
The month is March
```

In this example the `months` is a list. `months` is defined with the lines `months = ['January',` `'February'`, `'March'`, `'April'`, `'May'`, `'June'`, `'July'`,\ `'August'`, `'September'`, `'October'`, `'November'`, `'December']` (Note that a \ can be used to split a long line). The [and] start and end the list with comma's ("`,`") separating the list items. The list is used in `months[which_one - 1]`. A list consists of items that are numbered starting at 0. In other words if you wanted January you would type in 1 and that would have 1 subtracted off to use `months[0]`. Give a list a number and it will return the value that is stored at that location.

The statement `if 1 <= which_one <= 12:` will only be true if `which_one` is between one and twelve inclusive (in other words it is what you would expect if you have seen that in algebra). Since 1 is subtracted from `which_one` we get list locations from 0 to 11.

Lists can be thought of as a series of boxes. For example, the boxes created by `demolist = ['life', 42,` `'the'`, `'universe'`, `6`, `'and'`, `7]` would look like this:

box number	0	1	2	3	4	5	6
demolist	'life'	42	'the'	'universe'	6	'and'	7

Each box is referenced by its number so the statement `demolist[0]` would get `'life'`, `demolist[1]` would get 42 and so on up to `demolist[6]` getting 7.

8.2   More features of lists

The next example is just to show a lot of other stuff lists can do (for once, I don't expect you to type it in, but you should probably play around with lists until you are comfortable with them. Also, there will be another program that uses most of these features soon.). Here goes:

```
demolist = ['life', 42, 'the', 'universe', 6, 'and', 7]
print('demolist = ', demolist)
demolist.append('everything')
print("after 'everything' was appended demolist is now:")
print(demolist)
print('len(demolist) =', len(demolist))
print('demolist.index(42) =', demolist.index(42))
print('demolist[1] =', demolist[1])
#Next we will loop through the list
c = 0
while c < len(demolist):
    print('demolist[', c, ']=', demolist[c])
    c = c + 1
del demolist[2]
print("After 'the universe' was removed demolist is now:")
print(demolist)
if 'life' in demolist:
    print("'life' was found in demolist")
else:
    print("'life' was not found in demolist")
if 'amoeba' in demolist:
    print("'amoeba' was found in demolist")
if 'amoeba' not in demolist:
    print("'amoeba' was not found in demolist")
int_list = []
c = 0
while c < len(demolist):
    if type(0) == type(demolist[c]):
        int_list.append(demolist[c])
    c = c + 1
print('int_list is', int_list)
int_list.sort()
print('The sorted int_list is ', int_list)
```

The output is:

```
demolist =  ['life', 42, 'the', 'universe', 6, 'and', 7]
after 'everything' was appended demolist is now:
['life', 42, 'the', 'universe', 6, 'and', 7, 'everything']
len(demolist) = 8
demolist.index(42) = 1
demolist[1] = 42
demolist[ 0 ]= life
demolist[ 1 ]= 42
demolist[ 2 ]= the
demolist[ 3 ]= universe
demolist[ 4 ]= 6
demolist[ 5 ]= and
demolist[ 6 ]= 7
demolist[ 7 ]= everything
After 'the universe' was removed demolist is now:
['life', 42, 'universe', 6, 'and', 7, 'everything']
```

```
'life' was found in demolist
'amoeba' was not found in demolist
int_list is [42, 6, 7]
The sorted int_list is  [6, 7, 42]
```

This example uses a whole bunch of new functions. Notice that you can just `print` a whole list. Next the `append` function is used to add a new item to the end of the list. `len` returns how many items are in a list. The valid indexes (as in numbers that can be used inside of the []) of a list range from 0 to `len` − 1. The `index` function tell where the first location of an item is located in a list. Notice how `demolist.index(42)` returns 1 and when `demolist[1]` is run it returns 42. The line `#Next we will loop through the list` is a just a reminder to the programmer (also called a comment). Python will ignore any lines that start with a #. Next the lines:

```
c = 0
while c < len(demolist):
    print('demolist[', c, ']=', demolist[c])
    c = c + 1
```

This creates a variable `c` which starts at 0 and is incremented until it reaches the last index of the list. Meanwhile the `print` function prints out each element of the list.

The `del` command can be used to remove a given element in a list. The next few lines use the `in` operator to test if a element is in or is not in a list.

The `sort` function sorts the list. This is useful if you need a list in order from smallest number to largest or alphabetical. Note that this rearranges the list. Note also that the numbers were put in a new list, and that was sorted, instead of trying to sort a mixed list. Sorting numbers and strings does not really make sense and results in an error.

In summary for a list the following operations exist:

example	explanation
`list[2]`	accesses the element at index 2
`list[2] = 3`	sets the element at index 2 to be 3
`del list[2]`	removes the element at index 2
`len(list)`	returns the length of list
`"value" in list`	is true if `"value"` is an element in list
`"value" not in list`	is true if `"value"` is not an element in list
`list.sort()`	sorts list
`list.index("value")`	returns the index of the first place that `"value"` occurs
`list.append("value")`	adds an element `"value"` at the end of the list

This next example uses these features in a more useful way:

```
menu_item = 0
list = []
while menu_item != 9:
    print("--------------------")
    print("1. Print the list")
    print("2. Add a name to the list")
    print("3. Remove a name from the list")
    print("4. Change an item in the list")
    print("9. Quit")
    menu_item = int(input("Pick an item from the menu: "))
    if menu_item == 1:
        current = 0
        if len(list) > 0:
            while current < len(list):
                print(current, ". ", list[current])
```

```
                    current = current + 1
            else:
                print("List is empty")
        elif menu_item == 2:
            name = input("Type in a name to add: ")
            list.append(name)
        elif menu_item == 3:
            del_name = input("What name would you like to remove: ")
            if del_name in list:
                item_number = list.index(del_name)
                del list[item_number]
                #The code above only removes the first occurance of
                # the name.  The code below from Gerald removes all.
                #while del_name in list:
                #        item_number = list.index(del_name)
                #        del list[item_number]
            else:
                print(del_name, " was not found")
        elif menu_item == 4:
            old_name = input("What name would you like to change: ")
            if old_name in list:
                item_number = list.index(old_name)
                new_name = input("What is the new name: ")
                list[item_number] = new_name
            else:
                print(old_name, " was not found")
print("Goodbye")
```

And here is part of the output:

```
--------------------
1. Print the list
2. Add a name to the list
3. Remove a name from the list
4. Change an item in the list
9. Quit


Pick an item from the menu: 2
Type in a name to add: Jack

Pick an item from the menu: 2
Type in a name to add: Jill

Pick an item from the menu: 1
0 .  Jack
1 .  Jill

Pick an item from the menu: 3
What name would you like to remove: Jack

Pick an item from the menu: 4
What name would you like to change: Jill
What is the new name: Jill Peters
```

```
Pick an item from the menu: 1
0  .  Jill Peters

Pick an item from the menu: 9
Goodbye
```

That was a long program. Let's take a look at the source code. The line `list = []` makes the variable `list` a list with no items (or elements). The next important line is `while menu_item != 9:`. This line starts a loop that allows the menu system for this program. The next few lines display a menu and decide which part of the program to run.

The section:

```
current = 0
if len(list) > 0:
    while current < len(list):
        print(current, ". ", list[current])
        current = current + 1
else:
    print("List is empty")
```

goes through the list and prints each name. `len(list_name)` tell how many items are in a list. If `len` returns 0 then the list is empty.

Then a few lines later the statement `list.append(name)` appears. It uses the `append` function to add a item to the end of the list. Jump down another two lines and notice this section of code:

```
item_number = list.index(del_name)
del list[item_number]
```

Here the `index` function is used to find the index value that will be used later to remove the item. `del list[item_number]` is used to remove a element of the list.

The next section

```
old_name = input("What name would you like to change: ")
if old_name in list:
    item_number = list.index(old_name)
    new_name = input("What is the new name: ")
    list[item_number] = new_name
else:
    print(old_name, " was not found")
```

uses `index` to find the `item_number` and then puts `new_name` where the `old_name` was.

Congratulations, with lists under your belt, you now know enough of the language that you could do any computations that a computer can do (this is technically known as Turing-Completeness). Of course, there are still many features that are used to make your life easier.

8.3 Examples

test.py

```
## This program runs a test of knowledge

# First get the test questions
# Later this will be modified to use file io.
def get_questions():
    # notice how the data is stored as a list of lists
    return [["What color is the daytime sky on a clear day?", "blue"],\
            ["What is the answer to life, the universe and everything?", "42"],\
            ["What is a three letter word for mouse trap?", "cat"]]

# This will test a single question
# it takes a single question in
# it returns true if the user typed the correct answer, otherwise false
def check_question(question_and_answer):
    #extract the question and the answer from the list
    question = question_and_answer[0]
    answer = question_and_answer[1]
    # give the question to the user
    given_answer = input(question)
    # compare the user's answer to the tester's answer
    if answer == given_answer:
        print("Correct")
        return True
    else:
        print("Incorrect, correct was:", answer)
        return False

# This will run through all the questions
def run_test(questions):
    if len(questions) == 0:
        print("No questions were given.")
        # the return exits the function
        return
    index = 0
    right = 0
    while index < len(questions):
        #Check the question
        if check_question(questions[index]):
            right = right + 1
        #go to the next question
        index = index + 1
    #notice the order of the computation, first multiply, then divide
    print("You got ", right*100//len(questions), "% right out of", len(questions))

#now lets run the questions
run_test(get_questions())
```

Sample Output:

```
What color is the daytime sky on a clear day?green
Incorrect, correct was: blue
What is the answer to life, the universe and everything?42
Correct
What is a three letter word for mouse trap?cat
```

```
Correct
You got  66 % right out of 3
```

8.4 Exercises

Expand the test.py program so it has menu giving the option of taking the test, viewing the list of questions and answers, and an option to Quit. Also, add a new question to ask, "What noise does a truly advanced machine make?" with the answer of "ping".

For Loops

And here is the new typing exercise for this chapter:

```
onetoten = range(1, 11)
for count in onetoten:
    print(count)
```

and the ever-present output:

```
1
2
3
4
5
6
7
8
9
10
```

The output looks awfully familiar but the program code looks different. The first line uses the `range` function. The `range` function uses two arguments like this `range(start, finish)`. `start` is the first integer number that is produced. `finish` is one larger than the last number. If the `finish` number is not larger, than the `start` number, no numbers are produced. Note that this program could have been done in a shorter way:

```
for count in range(1, 11):
    print(count)
```

Here are some examples to show what happens with the `range` command (converted into a list with the `list` function):

```
>>> list(range(1, 10))
[1, 2, 3, 4, 5, 6, 7, 8, 9]
>>> list(range(-32, -20))
[-32, -31, -30, -29, -28, -27, -26, -25, -24, -23, -22, -21]
>>> list(range(5, 21))
[5, 6, 7, 8, 9, 10, 11, 12, 13, 14, 15, 16, 17, 18, 19, 20]
>>> list(range(21, 5))
[]
```

The next line `for count in onetoten:` uses the `for` control structure. A `for` control structure looks like `for` variable in list: . list is gone through starting with the first element of the list and going to the last.[1] As for goes through each element in a list it puts each into variable. That allows variable to be used in each successive time the for loop is run through. Here is another example (you don't have to type this) to demonstrate:

```
demolist = ['life', 42, 'the universe', 6, 'and', 7, 'everything']
for item in demolist:
    print("The Current item is:", item)
```

The output is:

```
The Current item is: life
The Current item is: 42
The Current item is: the universe
The Current item is: 6
The Current item is: and
The Current item is: 7
The Current item is: everything
```

Notice how the for loop goes through and sets item to each element in the list. So, what is for good for? (groan) The first use is to go through all the elements of a list and do something with each of them. Here a quick way to add up all the elements:

```
list = [2, 4, 6, 8]
sum = 0
for num in list:
    sum = sum + num
print("The sum is: ", sum)
```

with the output simply being:

```
The sum is:   20
```

Or you could write a program to find out if there are any duplicates in a list like this program does:

```
list = [4, 5, 7, 8, 9, 1, 0, 7, 10]
list.sort()
prev = list[0]
del list[0]
for item in list:
    if prev == item:
        print("Duplicate of ", prev, " Found")
    prev = item
```

and for good measure:

```
Duplicate of  7  Found
```

Okay, so how does it work? Here is a special debugging version to help you understand (you don't need to type this in):

---

[1] Technically range returns an iterator and for takes an iterator, which saves memory and is why the for loop does not need to have range converted to a list first.

```
l = [4, 5, 7, 8, 9, 1, 0, 7, 10]
print("l = [4, 5, 7, 8, 9, 1, 0, 7, 10]", "\tl:", l)
l.sort()
print("l.sort()", "\tl:", l)
prev = l[0]
print("prev = l[0]", "\tprev:", prev)
del l[0]
print("del l[0]", "\tl:", l)
for item in l:
    if prev == item:
        print("Duplicate of ", prev, " Found")
    print("if prev == item:", "\tprev:", prev, "\titem:", item)
    prev = item
    print("prev = item", "\t\tprev:", prev, "\titem:", item)
```

with the output being:

```
l = [4, 5, 7, 8, 9, 1, 0, 7, 10]  l: [4, 5, 7, 8, 9, 1, 0, 7, 10]
l.sort()  l: [0, 1, 4, 5, 7, 7, 8, 9, 10]
prev = l[0]  prev: 0
del l[0]  l: [1, 4, 5, 7, 7, 8, 9, 10]
if prev == item:  prev: 0  item: 1
prev = item  prev: 1  item: 1
if prev == item:  prev: 1  item: 4
prev = item  prev: 4  item: 4
if prev == item:  prev: 4  item: 5
prev = item  prev: 5  item: 5
if prev == item:  prev: 5  item: 7
prev = item  prev: 7  item: 7
Duplicate of  7  Found
if prev == item:  prev: 7  item: 7
prev = item  prev: 7  item: 7
if prev == item:  prev: 7  item: 8
prev = item  prev: 8  item: 8
if prev == item:  prev: 8  item: 9
prev = item  prev: 9  item: 9
if prev == item:  prev: 9  item: 10
prev = item  prev: 10  item: 10
```

The reason I put so many `print` functions in the code was so that you can see what is happening in each line. (BTW, if you can't figure out why a program is not working, try putting in lots of prints to you can see what is happening) First the program starts with a boring old list. Next the program sorts the list. This is so that any duplicates get put next to each other. The program then initializes a prev(ious) variable. Next the first element of the list is deleted so that the first item is not incorrectly thought to be a duplicate. Next a `for` loop is gone into. Each item of the list is checked to see if it is the same as the previous. If it is a duplicate was found. The value of prev is then changed so that the next time the `for` loop is run through prev is the previous item to the current. Sure enough, the 7 is found to be a duplicate. (Notice how \t is used to print a tab.)

The other way to use `for` loops is to do something a certain number of times. Here is some code to print out the first 11 numbers of the Fibonacci series:

```
a = 1
b = 1
for c in range(1, 10):
    print(a, end=" ")
```

```
n = a + b
a = b
b = n
```

with the surprising output (Notice how if you don't want `print` to go to the next line use the `end=" "` (i.e. if you want to print something else on that line).):

```
1 1 2 3 5 8 13 21 34
```

Everything that can be done with `for` loops can also be done with `while` loops but `for` loops give a easy way to go through all the elements in a list or to do something a certain number of times.

Boolean Expressions

Here is a little example of boolean expressions (you don't have to type it in):

```
a = 6
b = 7
c = 42
print(1, a == 6)
print(2, a == 7)
print(3, a == 6 and b == 7)
print(4, a == 7 and b == 7)
print(5, not a == 7)
print(6, a == 7 or b == 7)
print(7, a == 7 or b == 6)
print(8, not (a == 7 and b == 6))
print(9, not a == 7 and b == 6)
```

With the output being:

```
1 True
2 False
3 True
4 False
5 True
6 True
7 False
8 True
9 False
```

What is going on? The program consists of a bunch of funny looking `print` functions. Each `print` function prints a number and a expression. The number is to help keep track of which statement I am dealing with. Notice how each expression ends up being either True or False. The lines:

```
print(1, a == 6)
print(2, a == 7)
```

print out a True and a False respectively just as expected since the first is true since is 6 and the second is false since a is not 7. The third print, `print(3, a == 6 and b == 7)`, is a little different. The operator `and` means if both the statement before and the statement after are true then the whole expression is true otherwise the whole expression is false. The next line, `print(4, a == 7 and b == 7)`, shows how if part of an `and` expression is false, the whole thing is false. The behavior of `and` can be summarized as follows:

expression	result
true and true	true
true and false	false
false and true*	false
false and false*	false

*Notice that if the first expression is false Python does not check the second expression since it knows the whole expression is false.

The next line, `print(5, not a == 7)`, uses the `not` operator. `not` just gives the opposite of the expression (The expression could be rewritten as `print(5, a != 7)`). Here's the table:

expression	result
not true	false
not false	true

The two following lines, `print(6, a == 7 or b == 7)` and `print(7, a == 7 or b == 6)`, use the `or` operator. The `or` operator returns true if the first expression is true, or if the second expression is true or both are true. If neither are true it returns false. Here's the table:

expression	result
true or true*	true
true or false*	true
false or true	true
false or false	false

*Notice that if the first expression is true Python doesn't check the second expression since it knows the whole expression is true. This works since `or` is true if at least one half of the expression is true. The first part is true so the second part could be either false or true, but the whole expression is still true.

The next two lines, `print(8, not (a == 7 and b == 6))` and `print(9, not a == 7 and b == 6)`, show that parentheses can be used to group expressions and force one part to be evaluated first. Notice that the parentheses changed the expression from false to true. This occurred since the parentheses forced the `not` to apply to the whole expression instead of just the `a == 7` portion.

Here is an example of using a boolean expression:

```
list = ["Life", "The Universe", "Everything", "Jack", "Jill", "Life", "Jill"]

#make a copy of the list.  See the More on Lists chapter to explain what
#[:] means.
copy = list[:]
#sort the copy
copy.sort()
prev = copy[0]
del copy[0]

count = 0

#go through the list searching for a match
while count < len(copy) and copy[count] != prev:
    prev = copy[count]
    count = count + 1

#If a match was not found then count can't be < len
#since the while loop continues while count is < len
#and no match is found
if count < len(copy):
    print("First Match: ", prev)
```

And here is the output:

```
First Match:   Jill
```

This program works by continuing to check for match `while count < len(copy) and copy[count] !=`
`prev:`. When either `count` is greater than the last index of `copy` or a match has been found the `and` is no longer
true so the loop exits. The `if` simply checks to make sure that the `while` exited because a match was found.

The other 'trick' of `and` is used in this example. If you look at the table for `and` notice the * on the third and fourth
entries because these are not checked. If `count >= len(copy)` (in other words `count < len(copy)` is false)
then copy[count] is never looked at. This is because Python knows that if the first is false then they both can't be true.
This is known as a short circuit and is useful if the second half of the `and` will cause an error if something is wrong.
I used the first expression (`count < len(copy)`) to check and see if `count` was a valid index for `copy`. (If you
don't believe me remove the matches 'Jill' and 'Life', check that it still works and then reverse the order of `count <`
`len(copy) and copy[count] != prev` to `copy[count] != prev and count < len(copy)`.)

Boolean expressions can be used when you need to check two or more different things at once.

10.1   Examples

password1.py

```
## This programs asks a user for a name and a password.
# It then checks them to make sure the the user is allowed in.

name = input("What is your name? ")
password = input("What is the password? ")
if name == "Josh" and password == "Friday":
    print("Welcome Josh")
elif name == "Fred" and password == "Rock":
    print("Welcome Fred")
else:
    print("I don't know you.")
```

Sample runs

```
What is your name? Josh
What is the password? Friday
Welcome Josh

What is your name? Bill
What is the password? Money
I don't know you.
```

10.2   Exercises

Write a program that has a user guess your name, but they only get 3 chances to do so until the program quits.

Dictionaries

This chapter is about dictionaries. Dictionaries have keys and values. The keys are used to find the values. Here is an interactive mode demonstration of creating a phone numbers dictionary:

```
>>> #Create a dictionary
... numbers = {}
>>> #Add some numbers
... numbers["Joe"] = "545-4464"
>>> numbers["Jill"] = "979-4654"
>>> #Look up a number
... numbers["Joe"]
'545-4464'
```

Here is an example of a program that makes a phone numbers dictionary:

```
def print_menu():
    print('1. Print Phone Numbers')
    print('2. Add a Phone Number')
    print('3. Remove a Phone Number')
    print('4. Lookup a Phone Number')
    print('5. Quit')
    print()
numbers = {}
menu_choice = 0
print_menu()
while menu_choice != 5:
    menu_choice = int(input("Type in a number (1-5):"))
    if menu_choice == 1:
        print("Telephone Numbers:")
        for x in sorted(numbers.keys()):
            print("Name: ", x, " \tNumber: ", numbers[x])
        print()
    elif menu_choice == 2:
        print("Add Name and Number")
        name = input("Name:")
        phone = input("Number:")
        numbers[name] = phone
    elif menu_choice == 3:
        print("Remove Name and Number")
        name = input("Name:")
        if name in numbers:
```

```
            del numbers[name]
        else:
            print(name, " was not found")
    elif menu_choice == 4:
        print("Lookup Number")
        name = input("Name:")
        if name in numbers:
            print("The number is", numbers[name])
        else:
            print(name, " was not found")
    elif menu_choice != 5:
        print_menu()
```

And here is my output:

```
1. Print Phone Numbers
2. Add a Phone Number
3. Remove a Phone Number
4. Lookup a Phone Number
5. Quit

Type in a number (1-5):2
Add Name and Number
Name:Joe
Number:545-4464
Type in a number (1-5):2
Add Name and Number
Name:Jill
Number:979-4654
Type in a number (1-5):2
Add Name and Number
Name:Fred
Number:132-9874
Type in a number (1-5):1
Telephone Numbers:
Name:  Fred     Number:  132-9874
Name:  Jill     Number:  979-4654
Name:  Joe      Number:  545-4464

Type in a number (1-5):4
Lookup Number
Name:Joe
The number is 545-4464
Type in a number (1-5):3
Remove Name and Number
Name:Fred
Type in a number (1-5):1
Telephone Numbers:
Name:  Jill     Number:  979-4654
Name:  Joe      Number:  545-4464

Type in a number (1-5):5
```

This program is similar to the name list earlier in the the chapter on lists. Here's how the program works. First, the function `print_menu` is defined. `print_menu` just prints a menu that is later used twice in the program. Next comes the funny looking line `numbers = {}`. All that line does is tell Python that `numbers` is a dictionary. The next few lines just make the menu work. The lines:

```
for x in sorted(numbers.keys()):
    print("Name: ", x, " \tNumber: ", numbers[x])
```

go through the dictionary and print all the information. The function `numbers.keys()` returns a list that is then used by the `for` loop. The list returned by `keys` is not in any particular order so if you want it in alphabetic order it must be sorted as is done with the `sorted` function. Similar to lists the statement `numbers[x]` is used to access a specific member of the dictionary. Of course in this case `x` is a string. Next the line `numbers[name] = phone` adds a name and phone number to the dictionary. If `name` had already been in the dictionary `phone` would replace whatever was there before. Next the lines:

```
if name in numbers:
    del numbers[name]
```

see if a name is in the dictionary and remove it if it is. The function `name in numbers` returns true if `name` is in `numbers` but otherwise returns false. The line `del numbers[name]` removes the key `name` and the value associated with that key. The lines:

```
if name in numbers:
    print("The number is", numbers[name])
```

check to see if the dictionary has a certain key and if it does prints out the number associated with it. Lastly, if the menu choice is invalid it reprints the menu for your viewing pleasure.

A recap: Dictionaries have keys and values. Keys can be strings or numbers. Keys point to values. Values can be any type of variable (including lists or even dictionaries (those dictionaries or lists of course can contain dictionaries or lists themselves (scary right? :)))). Here is an example of using a list in a dictionary:

```
max_points = [25, 25, 50, 25, 100]
assignments = ['hw ch 1', 'hw ch 2', 'quiz    ', 'hw ch 3', 'test']
students = {'#Max':max_points}

def print_menu():
    print("1. Add student")
    print("2. Remove student")
    print("3. Print grades")
    print("4. Record grade")
    print("5. Print Menu")
    print("6. Exit")

def print_all_grades():
    print('\t', end=' ')
    for i in range(len(assignments)):
        print(assignments[i], '\t', end=' ')
    print()
    keys = list(students.keys())
    keys.sort()
    for x in keys:
        print(x, '\t', end=' ')
        grades = students[x]
        print_grades(grades)
```

```
def print_grades(grades):
    for i in range(len(grades)):
        print(grades[i], '\t\t', end=' ')
    print()

print_menu()
menu_choice = 0
while menu_choice != 6:
    print()
    menu_choice = int(input("Menu Choice (1-6):"))
    if menu_choice == 1:
        name = input("Student to add:")
        students[name] = [0]*len(max_points)
    elif menu_choice == 2:
        name = input("Student to remove:")
        if name in students:
            del students[name]
        else:
            print("Student: ", name, " not found")
    elif menu_choice == 3:
        print_all_grades()

    elif menu_choice == 4:
        print("Record Grade")
        name = input("Student:")
        if name in students:
            grades = students[name]
            print("Type in the number of the grade to record")
            print("Type a 0 (zero) to exit")
            for i in range(len(assignments)):
                print(i+1, ' ', assignments[i], '\t', end=' ')
            print()
            print_grades(grades)
            which = 1234
            while which != -1:
                which = int(input("Change which Grade:"))
                which = which-1
                if 0 <= which < len(grades):
                    grade = int(input("Grade:"))
                    grades[which] = grade
                elif which != -1:
                    print("Invalid Grade Number")
        else:
            print("Student not found")
    elif menu_choice != 6:
        print_menu()
```

and here is a sample output:

```
1. Add student
2. Remove student
3. Print grades
4. Record grade
```

```
5. Print Menu
6. Exit

Menu Choice (1-6):3
          hw ch 1          hw ch 2          quiz          hw ch 3          test
#Max      25               25               50            25               100


Menu Choice (1-6):5
1. Add student
2. Remove student
3. Print grades
4. Record grade
5. Print Menu
6. Exit

Menu Choice (1-6):1
Student to add:Bill


Menu Choice (1-6):4
Record Grade
Student:Bill
Type in the number of the grade to record
Type a 0 (zero) to exit
1  hw ch 1      2  hw ch 2      3  quiz      4  hw ch 3      5  test
0                0              0            0               0
Change which Grade:1
Grade:25
Change which Grade:2
Grade:24
Change which Grade:3
Grade:45
Change which Grade:4
Grade:23
Change which Grade:5
Grade:95
Change which Grade:0


Menu Choice (1-6):3
          hw ch 1          hw ch 2          quiz          hw ch 3          test
#Max      25               25               50            25               100
Bill      25               24               45            23               95

Menu Choice (1-6):6
```

Here's how the program works. Basically, the variable students is a dictionary with the keys being the name of the students and the values being their grades. The first two lines just create two lists. The next line students = {'#Max':max_points} creates a new dictionary with the key #Max and the value is set to be [25, 25, 50, 25, 100] (since thats what max_points was when the assignment is made) (I use the key #Max since # is sorted ahead of any alphabetic characters). Next, print_menu is defined. Then, the print_all_grades function is defined in the lines:

```
def print_all_grades():
    print('\t', end=' ')
    for i in range(len(assignments)):
        print(assignments[i], '\t', end=' ')
    print()
    keys = list(students.keys())
    keys.sort()
    for x in keys:
        print(x, '\t', end=' ')
        grades = students[x]
        print_grades(grades)
```

Notice how first the keys are gotten out of the `students` dictionary with the `keys` function in the line `keys = list(students.keys())` The result of `keys()` is converted into a list so all the functions for lists can be used on it. Next, the keys are sorted in the line `keys.sort()` since it is a list. `for` is used to go through all the keys. The grades are stored as a list inside the dictionary so the assignment `grades = students[x]` gives `grades` the list that is stored at the key x. The function `print_grades` just prints a list and is defined a few lines later.

The later lines of the program implement the various options of the menu. The line `students[name] = [0]*len(max_points)` adds a student to the key of their name. The notation `[0]*len(max_points)` just creates a array of 0's that is the same length as the `max_points` list.

The remove student entry just deletes a student similar to the telephone book example. The record grades choice is a little more complex. The grades are retrieved in the line `grades = students[name]`, which gets a reference to the grades of the student `name`. A grade is then recorded in the line `grades[which] = grade`. You may notice that `grades` is never put back into the students dictionary (as in no `students[name] = grades`). The reason for the missing statement is that `grades` is actually another name for `students[name]` and so changing `grades` changes `student[name]`.

Dictionaries provide a easy way to link keys to values. This can be used to easily keep track of data that is attached to various keys.

Using Modules

Here's this chapter's typing exercise (name it cal.py)[1]:

```
import calendar

year = int(input("Type in the year number:"))
calendar.prcal(year)
```

And here is part of the output I got:

```
Type in the year number:2001
                        2001

        January                 February                 March
Mo Tu We Th Fr Sa Su    Mo Tu We Th Fr Sa Su    Mo Tu We Th Fr Sa Su
 1  2  3  4  5  6  7              1  2  3  4              1  2  3  4
 8  9 10 11 12 13 14     5  6  7  8  9 10 11     5  6  7  8  9 10 11
15 16 17 18 19 20 21    12 13 14 15 16 17 18    12 13 14 15 16 17 18
22 23 24 25 26 27 28    19 20 21 22 23 24 25    19 20 21 22 23 24 25
29 30 31                26 27 28                26 27 28 29 30 31
```

(I skipped some of the output, but I think you get the idea.) So what does the program do? The first line `import calendar` uses a new command `import`. The command `import` loads a module (in this case the `calendar` module). To see the commands available in the standard modules either look in the library reference for python (if you downloaded it) or go to `https://docs.python.org/3/library/index.html`. The calendar module is described in 8.2. If you look at the documentation it lists a function called `prcal` that prints a calendar for a year. The line `calendar.prcal(year)` uses the function. In summary to use a module `import` it and then use `module_name.function` for functions in the module. Another way to write the program is:

```
from calendar import prcal

year = int(input("Type in the year number:"))
prcal(year)
```

This version imports a specific function from a module. Here is another program that uses the Python Library (name it something like clock.py) (press Ctrl and the 'c' key at the same time to kill the program):

---

[1] import actually looks for a file named calendar.py and reads it in. If the file is named calendar.py and it sees a 'import calendar' it tries to read in itself which works poorly at best.

```
from time import time, ctime

prev_time = ""
while(1):
    the_time = ctime(time())
    if(prev_time != the_time):
        print("The time is:", ctime(time()))
        prev_time = the_time
```

With some output being:

```
The time is: Sun Aug 20 13:40:04 2000
The time is: Sun Aug 20 13:40:05 2000
The time is: Sun Aug 20 13:40:06 2000
The time is: Sun Aug 20 13:40:07 2000
Traceback (innermost last):
  File "clock.py", line 5, in ?
    the_time = ctime(time())
KeyboardInterrupt
```

The output will keep coming forever (or at least until the heat death of the computer) so of course so I canceled it with a Ctrl+C. The program just does a infinite loop and each time checks to see if the time has changed and prints it if it has. Notice how multiple names after the import statement are used in the line from time import time, ctime.

The Python Library contains many useful functions. These functions give your programs more abilities and many of them can simplify programming in Python.

12.1 Exercises

Rewrite the high_low.py program from section 5.2 to use the last two digits of time at that moment to be the 'random' number.

More on Lists

We have already seen lists and how they can be used. Now that you have some more background I will go into more detail about lists. First we will look at more ways to get at the elements in a list and then we will talk about copying them.

Here are some examples of using indexing to access a single element of an list:

```
>>> list = ['zero', 'one', 'two', 'three', 'four', 'five']
>>> list[0]
'zero'
>>> list[4]
'four'
>>> list[5]
'five'
```

All those examples should look familiar to you. If you want the first item in the list just look at index 0. The second item is index 1 and so on through the list. However, what if you want the last item in the list? One way could be to use the len function like list[len(list)-1]. This way works since the len function always returns the last index plus one. The second from the last would then be list[len(list)-2]. There is an easier way to do this. In Python the last item is always index -1. The second to the last is index -2 and so on. Here are some more examples:

```
>>> list[len(list)-1]
'five'
>>> list[len(list)-2]
'four'
>>> list[-1]
'five'
>>> list[-2]
'four'
>>> list[-6]
'zero'
```

Thus any item in the list can be indexed in two ways: from the front and from the back.

Another useful way to get into parts of lists is using slices. Here is another example to give you an idea what they can be used for:

```
>>> list = [0, 'Fred', 2, 'S.P.A.M.', 'Stocking', 42, "Jack", "Jill"]
>>> list[0]
0
>>> list[7]
'Jill'
```

```
>>> list[0:8]
[0, 'Fred', 2, 'S.P.A.M.', 'Stocking', 42, 'Jack', 'Jill']
>>> list[2:4]
[2, 'S.P.A.M.']
>>> list[4:7]
['Stocking', 42, 'Jack']
>>> list[1:5]
['Fred', 2, 'S.P.A.M.', 'Stocking']
```

Slices are used to return part of a list. The slice operator is in the form
list[first_index:following_index]. The slice goes from the first_index to the index before
the following_index. You can use both types of indexing:

```
>>> list[-4:-2]
['Stocking', 42]
>>> list[-4]
'Stocking'
>>> list[-4:6]
['Stocking', 42]
```

Another trick with slices is the unspecified index. If the first index is not specified the beginning of the list is assumed.
If the following index is not specified the whole rest of the list is assumed. Here are some examples:

```
>>> list[:2]
[0, 'Fred']
>>> list[-2:]
['Jack', 'Jill']
>>> list[:3]
[0, 'Fred', 2]
>>> list[:-5]
[0, 'Fred', 2]
```

Here is a program example:

```
poem = ["<B>", "Jack", "and", "Jill", "</B>", "went", "up", "the", "hill",\
        "to", "<B>", "fetch", "a", "pail", "of", "</B>", "water.", "Jack",\
        "fell", "<B>", "down", "and", "broke", "</B>", "his", "crown", "and",\
        "<B>", "Jill", "came", "</B>", "tumbling", "after"]

def get_bolds(list):
    ## is_bold tells whether or not the we are currently looking at
    ## a bold section of text.
    is_bold = False
    ## start_block is the index of the start of either an unbolded
    ## segment of text or a bolded segment.
    start_block = 0
    for index in range(len(list)):
        ##Handle a starting of bold text
        if list[index] == "<B>":
            if is_bold:
                print("Error:  Extra Bold")
            ##print "Not Bold:", list[start_block:index]
            is_bold = True
            start_block = index+1
```

```
            ##Handle end of bold text
            ##Remember that the last number in a slice is the index
            ## after the last index used.
            if list[index] == "</B>":
                if not is_bold:
                    print("Error: Extra Close Bold")
                print("Bold [", start_block, ":", index, "] ",\
                list[start_block:index])
                is_bold = False
                start_block = index+1

get_bolds(poem)
```

with the output being:

```
Bold [ 1 : 4 ]    ['Jack', 'and', 'Jill']
Bold [ 11 : 15 ]    ['fetch', 'a', 'pail', 'of']
Bold [ 20 : 23 ]    ['down', 'and', 'broke']
Bold [ 28 : 30 ]    ['Jill', 'came']
```

The get_bold function takes in a list that is broken into words and token's. The tokens that it looks for are <B> which starts the bold text and <\B> which ends bold text. The function get_bold goes through and searches for the start and end tokens.

The next feature of lists is copying them. If you try something simple like:

```
>>> a = [1, 2, 3]
>>> b = a
>>> print(b)
[1, 2, 3]
>>> b[1] = 10
>>> print(b)
[1, 10, 3]
>>> print(a)
[1, 10, 3]
```

This probably looks surprising since a modification to b resulted in a being changed as well. What happened is that the statement b = a makes b a *reference* to the same list that a is a reference to. This means that b and a are different names for the same list. Hence any modification to b changes a as well. However some assignments don't create two names for one list:

```
>>> a = [1, 2, 3]
>>> b = a*2
>>> print(a)
[1, 2, 3]
>>> print(b)
[1, 2, 3, 1, 2, 3]
>>> a[1] = 10
>>> print(a)
[1, 10, 3]
>>> print(b)
[1, 2, 3, 1, 2, 3]
```

In this case, b is not a reference to a since the expression a*2 creates a new list. Then the statement b = a*2 gives b a reference to a*2 rather than a reference to a. All assignment operations create a reference. When you pass a list as a argument to a function you create a reference as well. Most of the time you don't have to worry about creating references rather than copies. However when you need to make modifications to one list without changing another name of the list you have to make sure that you have actually created a copy.

There are several ways to make a copy of a list. The simplest that works most of the time is the slice operator since it always makes a new list even if it is a slice of a whole list:

```
>>> a = [1, 2, 3]
>>> b = a[:]
>>> b[1] = 10
>>> print(a)
[1, 2, 3]
>>> print(b)
[1, 10, 3]
```

Taking the slice [:] creates a new copy of the list. However it only copies the outer list. Any sublist inside is still a references to the sublist in the original list. Therefore, when the list contains lists the inner lists have to be copied as well. You could do that manually but Python already contains a module to do it. You use the deepcopy function of the copy module:

```
>>> import copy
>>> a = [[1, 2, 3], [4, 5, 6]]
>>> b = a[:]
>>> c = copy.deepcopy(a)
>>> b[0][1] = 10
>>> c[1][1] = 12
>>> print(a)
[[1, 10, 3], [4, 5, 6]]
>>> print(b)
[[1, 10, 3], [4, 5, 6]]
>>> print(c)
[[1, 2, 3], [4, 12, 6]]
```

First of all, notice that a is an array of arrays. Then notice that when b[0][1] = 10 is run both a and b are changed, but c is not. This happens because the inner arrays are still references when the slice operator is used. However, with deepcopy, c was fully copied.

So, should I worry about references every time I use a function or =? The good news is that you only have to worry about references when using dictionaries and lists. Numbers and strings create references when assigned but every operation on numbers and strings that modifies them creates a new copy so you can never modify them unexpectedly. You do have to think about references when you are modifying a list or a dictionary.

By now you are probably wondering why are references used at all? The basic reason is speed. It is much faster to make a reference to a thousand element list than to copy all the elements. The other reason is that it allows you to have a function to modify the inputed list or dictionary. Just remember about references if you ever have some weird problem with data being changed when it shouldn't be.

Revenge of the Strings

And now presenting a cool trick that can be done with strings:

```python
def shout(string):
    for character in string:
        print("Gimme a "+character)
        print("'"+character+"'")

shout("Lose")

def middle(string):
    print("The middle character is:", string[len(string)//2])

middle("abcdefg")
middle("The Python Programming Language")
middle("Atlanta")
```

And the output is:

```
Gimme a L
'L'
Gimme a o
'o'
Gimme a s
's'
Gimme a e
'e'
The middle character is: d
The middle character is: r
The middle character is: a
```

What these programs demonstrate is that strings are similar to lists in several ways. The shout procedure shows that for loops can be used with strings just as they can be used with lists. The middle procedure shows that that strings can also use the len function and array indexes and slices. Most list features work on strings as well.

The next program demonstrates some string specific features:

```python
def to_upper(string):
    ## Converts a string to upper case
    upper_case = ""
    for character in string:
```

```
            if 'a' <= character <= 'z':
                location = ord(character) - ord('a')
                new_ascii = location + ord('A')
                character = chr(new_ascii)
            upper_case = upper_case + character
        return upper_case

print(to_upper("This is Text"))
```

with the output being:

```
THIS IS TEXT
```

This works because the computer represents the characters of a string as numbers from 0 to 255 (or more if they are Unicode). Python has a function called `ord` (short for ordinal) that returns a character as a number. There is also a corresponding function called `chr` that converts a number into a character. With this in mind, the program should start to be clear. The first detail is the line: `if 'a' <= character <= 'z':` which checks to see if a letter is lower case. If it is, then the next lines are used. First it is converted into a location so that a=0, b=1, c=2 and so on with the line: `location = ord(character) - ord('a')`. Next the new value is found with `new_ascii = location + ord('A')`. This value is converted back to a character that is now upper case. And for what it is worth, Python does have a built-in string functions `upper` and `lower` for making upper and lower case strings.

Now for some interactive typing exercise:

```
>>> #Integer to String
...
>>> 2
2
>>> str(2)
'2'
>>> -123
-123
>>> str(-123)
'-123'

>>> #String to Integer
...
>>> "23"
'23'
>>> int("23")
23
>>> "23"*2
'2323'
>>> int("23")*2
46
>>> int(23.4)
23

>>> #Float to String
...
>>> 1.23
1.23
>>> str(1.23)
'1.23'
```

```
>>> #Float to Integer
...
>>> 1.23
1.23
>>> int(1.23)
1
>>> int(-1.23)
-1

>>> #String to Float
...
>>> float("1.23")
1.23
>>> "1.23"
'1.23'
>>> float("123")
123.0
```

If you haven't guessed already, the function `str` can convert a integer to a string and the function `int` can convert a string (or a float) to an integer. The function `float` can convert a string (or an integer) to a float. The `str` function returns a printable representation of something. Here are some examples of this:

```
>>> str(1)
'1'
>>> str(234.14)
'234.14'
>>> str([4, 42, 10])
'[4, 42, 10]'
```

One useful string function is the `split` function that is part of any string. Here's the example:

```
>>> "This is a bunch of words".split()
['This', 'is', 'a', 'bunch', 'of', 'words']
>>> "First batch, second batch, third, fourth".split(",")
['First batch', ' second batch', ' third', ' fourth']
```

Notice how `split` converts a string into a list of strings. The string is split by spaces by default or by the optional second argument (in this case, a comma).

One more feature is worth mentioning. Python strings can have escape sequences that allow characters that otherwise might be hard to insert in a string. Here is a table giving some examples:

Escape	What it makes
\'	'
\"	"
\\	\
\n	newline
\t	tab
\x6A	j (lets a character be specified by a hex byte)
\u2661	♡
\U00002661	♡
\N{white heart suit}	♡

14.1 Examples

```
#This program requires a excellent understanding of decimal numbers
def to_string(in_int):
    "Converts an integer to a string"
    out_str = ""
    prefix = ""
    if in_int < 0:
        prefix = "-"
        in_int = -in_int
    while in_int // 10 != 0:
        out_str = chr(ord('0')+in_int % 10) + out_str
        in_int = in_int // 10
    out_str = chr(ord('0')+in_int % 10) + out_str
    return prefix + out_str

def to_int(in_str):
    "Converts a string to an integer"
    out_num = 0
    if in_str[0] == "-":
        multiplier = -1
        in_str = in_str[1:]
    else:
        multiplier = 1
    for x in range(0, len(in_str)):
        out_num = out_num * 10 + ord(in_str[x]) - ord('0')
    return out_num * multiplier

print(to_string(2))
print(to_string(23445))
print(to_string(-23445))
print(to_int("14234"))
print(to_int("-3512"))
```

The output is:

```
2
23445
-23445
14234
-3512
```

File IO

Here is a simple example of file IO:

```
#Write a file
out_file = open("test.txt", "w")
out_file.write("This Text is going to out file\nLook at it and see\n")
out_file.close()

#Read a file
in_file = open("test.txt", "r")
text = in_file.read()
in_file.close()

print(text)
```

The output and the contents of the file test.txt are:

```
This Text is going to out file
Look at it and see
```

Notice that it wrote a file called test.txt in the directory that you ran the program from. The \n in the string tells Python to put a **n**ewline where it is.

A overview of file IO is:

1. Get a file object with the open function.

2. Read or write to the file object (depending on if you open it with a "r" or "w")

3. Close it

The first step is to get a file object. The way to do this is to use the open function. The format is file_object = open(filename, mode) where file_object is the variable to put the file object, filename is a string with the filename, and mode is either "r" to read a file or "w" to write a file. Next the file object's functions can be called. The two most common functions are read and write. The write function adds a string to the end of the file. The read function reads the next thing in the file and returns it as a string. If no argument is given it will return the whole file (as done in the example).

Now here is a new version of the phone numbers program that we made earlier:

```
def print_numbers(numbers):
```

```python
    print("Telephone Numbers:")
    for x in numbers:
        print("Name: ", x, " \tNumber: ", numbers[x])
    print()

def add_number(numbers, name, number):
    numbers[name] = number

def lookup_number(numbers, name):
    if name in numbers:
        return "The number is "+numbers[name]
    else:
        return name+" was not found"

def remove_number(numbers, name):
    if name in numbers:
        del numbers[name]
    else:
        print(name, " was not found")


def load_numbers(numbers, filename):
    in_file = open(filename, "r")
    while True:
        in_line = in_file.readline()
        if in_line == "":
            break
        in_line = in_line[:-1]
        [name, number] = in_line.split(",")
        numbers[name] = number
    in_file.close()

def save_numbers(numbers, filename):
    out_file = open(filename, "w")
    for x in numbers:
        out_file.write(x+","+numbers[x]+"\n")
    out_file.close()


def print_menu():
    print('1. Print Phone Numbers')
    print('2. Add a Phone Number')
    print('3. Remove a Phone Number')
    print('4. Lookup a Phone Number')
    print('5. Load numbers')
    print('6. Save numbers')
    print('7. Quit')
    print()

phone_list = {}
menu_choice = 0
print_menu()
while menu_choice != 7:
    menu_choice = int(input("Type in a number (1-7):"))
```

```
    if menu_choice == 1:
        print_numbers(phone_list)
    elif menu_choice == 2:
        print("Add Name and Number")
        name = input("Name:")
        phone = input("Number:")
        add_number(phone_list, name, phone)
    elif menu_choice == 3:
        print("Remove Name and Number")
        name = input("Name:")
        remove_number(phone_list, name)
    elif menu_choice == 4:
        print("Lookup Number")
        name = input("Name:")
        print(lookup_number(phone_list, name))
    elif menu_choice == 5:
        filename = input("Filename to load:")
        load_numbers(phone_list, filename)
    elif menu_choice == 6:
        filename = input("Filename to save:")
        save_numbers(phone_list, filename)
    elif menu_choice == 7:
        pass
    else:
        print_menu()
print("Goodbye")
```

Notice that it now includes saving and loading files. Here is some output of my running it twice:

```
> python3 tele2.py
1. Print Phone Numbers
2. Add a Phone Number
3. Remove a Phone Number
4. Lookup a Phone Number
5. Load numbers
6. Save numbers
7. Quit

Type in a number (1-7):2
Add Name and Number
Name:Jill
Number:1234
Type in a number (1-7):2
Add Name and Number
Name:Fred
Number:4321
Type in a number (1-7):1
Telephone Numbers:
Name:  Jill      Number:  1234
Name:  Fred      Number:  4321

Type in a number (1-7):6
Filename to save:numbers.txt
Type in a number (1-7):7
```

```
Goodbye

> python3 tele2.py
1. Print Phone Numbers
2. Add a Phone Number
3. Remove a Phone Number
4. Lookup a Phone Number
5. Load numbers
6. Save numbers
7. Quit

Type in a number (1-7):5
Filename to load:numbers.txt
Type in a number (1-7):1
Telephone Numbers:
Name:  Jill      Number:  1234
Name:  Fred      Number:  4321

Type in a number (1-7):7
Goodbye
```

The new portions of this program are:

```
def load_numbers(numbers, filename):
    in_file = open(filename, "r")
    while True:
        in_line = in_file.readline()
        if len(in_line) == 0:
            break
        in_line = in_line[:-1]
        [name, number] = in_line.split(",")
        numbers[name] = number
    in_file.close()


def save_numbers(numbers, filename):
    out_file = open(filename, "w")
    for x in numbers:
        out_file.write(x+","+numbers[x]+"\n")
    out_file.close()
```

First we will look at the save portion of the program. First, it creates a file object with the command `open(filename, "w")`. Next, it goes through and creates a line for each of the phone numbers with the command `out_file.write(x+","+numbers[x]+"\n")`. This writes out a line that contains the name, a comma, the number and follows it by a newline.

The loading portion is a little more complicated. It starts by getting a file object. Then, it uses a `while True:` loop to keep looping until a `break` statement is encountered. Next, it gets a line with the line `in_line = in_file.readline()`. The `readline` function will return a empty string (len(string) == 0) when the end of the file is reached. The `if` statement checks for this and `break`s out of the `while` loop when that happens. Of course if the `readline` function did not return the newline at the end of the line there would be no way to tell if an empty string was an empty line or the end of the file so the newline is left in what `readline` returns. Hence we have to get rid of the newline. The line `in_line = in_line[:-1]` does this for us by dropping the last character. Next the line `[name, number] = string.split(in_line, ",")` splits the line at the comma into a name and a number. This is then added to the `numbers` dictionary.

15.1 Exercises

Now modify the grades program from section 11 so that it uses file IO to keep a record of the students.

Dealing with the imperfect (or how to handle errors)

So you now have the perfect program, it runs flawlessly, except for one detail. It will crash on invalid user input. Have no fear, for Python has a special control structure for you. It's called `try` and it tries to do something. Here is an example of a program with a problem:

```python
print("Type Control C or -1 to exit")
number = 1
while number != -1:
    number = int(input("Enter a number: "))
    print("You entered: ", number)
```

Notice how when you enter @#& it outputs something like:

```
Traceback (most recent call last):
  File "notry.py", line 8, in <module>
    number = int(input("Enter a number: "))
ValueError: invalid literal for int() with base 10: '@#&'
```

As you can see, the `int` function is unhappy with the number @#& (as well it should be). The last line shows what the problem is; Python found a `ValueError`. How can our program deal with this? What we do is first: put the place where the errors occurs in a `try` block, and second: tell Python how we want `ValueErrors` handled. The following program does this:

```python
print("Type Control C or -1 to exit")
number = 1
while number != -1:
    try:
        number = int(input("Enter a number: "))
        print("You entered: ", number)
    except ValueError:
        print("That was not a number")
```

Now when we run the new program and give it @#& it tells us "That was not a number." and continues with what it was doing before.

When your program keeps having some error that you know how to handle, put code in a `try` block, and put the way to handle the error in the `except` block.

16.1   Exercises

Update at least the phone numbers program so it doesn't crash if a user doesn't enter any data at the menu.

SEVENTEEN

The End

Hopefully, you should be able to program in Python now. There is a version of this tutorial on Wikibooks: `https://en.wikibooks.org/wiki/Non-Programmer's_Tutorial_for_Python_3` which are based on this tutorial. You probably can also now understand the The Python Tutorial by Guido van Rossum at `https://docs.python.org/3/tutorial/index.html`

This tutorial has been written on and off since 1999. Thanks to everyone who has emailed me. If you have comments, feel free to add them to the talk pages on the wikibooks version or email me.

Happy programming, may it change your life and the world.

FAQ

Is there an updated version? Maybe, take a look at the webpage: `http://jjc.freeshell.org/easytut3/` and the wikibooks version:
`https://en.wikibooks.org/wiki/Non-Programmer's_Tutorial_for_Python_3`

Is there a printable version? Yes, see the next question.

Is there a PDF or zipped version? Yes, go to `http://jjc.freeshell.org/easytut3/` for several different versions.

What is the tutorial written with? LaTeX, see the `easytut3.tex` file.

I can't type in programs of more than one line. If the programs that you type in run as soon as you are typing them in, you need to edit a file instead of typing them in interactive mode. (Hint: interactive mode is the mode with the `>>>` prompt in front of it.)

My question is not answered here. Email me and ask. Please send me source code if at all relevant (even (or maybe especially), if it doesn't work). Helpful things to include are: what you were trying to do, what happened, what you expected to happen, error messages, version of Python, Operating System, and whether or not your cat was stepping on the keyboard. (The cat in my house has a fondness for space bars and control keys.)

I want to read it in a different language. There are several translations of the Python 2 version that I know of, but none of the Python 3 version yet. One is in Korean and is available at: `http://jjc.freeshell.org/easytut/korean/`. Another is in Spanish and at: `http://jjc.freeshell.org/easytut/easytut_es/`. Another is in Italian and is available at `http://jjc.freeshell.org/easytut/easytut_it/`. Another is in Greek and available at `http://jjc.freeshell.org/easytut/easytut_gr/`. Another is in Russian and is available at `http://jjc.freeshell.org/easytut/Easytut_Russian/` Several people have said they are doing a translation in other languages such as French, but I never heard back from them. If you have done a translation or know of any translations, please either send it to me or send me a link.

How do I make a GUI in Python? You can use either TKinter at `https://docs.python.org/3/library/tk.html` or WXPython at `http://www.wxpython.org/`

How do I make a game in Python? The best method is probably to use PYgame at `http://pygame.org/`

How do I make an exectable from a Python program? Short answer: Python is an interepreted language so that is impossible. Long answer is that something similar to an executable can be created by taking the Python interpreter and the file and joining them together and distributing that. For Windows, one solution to do this is `http://www.py2exe.org/` On Unix (Such as Linux or macOS) you can just start the program with `#!/usr/bin/env python3` and make the file executable `chmod +x file.py`

I need help with the exercises Hint, the password program requires two variables, one to keep track of the number of times the password was typed in, and another to keep track of the last password typed in. Also, you can download solutions from `http://jjc.freeshell.org/easytut3/`

www.ingramcontent.com/pod-product-compliance
Lightning Source LLC
Chambersburg PA
CBHW081209180526
45170CB00006B/2280